What others are saying about *Raising Well-Behaved Kids*.

I have been in awe of Sue since we first met. Her 5 children are all bright, charming, well-mannered and well-rounded young people. Not only did Sue do a wonderful job with her kids, but she did it while running a business, maintaining a smooth-running household, and home schooling. Sue is truly gifted – I can hardly wait for her to finish her book so I can share in her secrets!

T. Kuehn
lawyer and parent

For those parents who believe that kids don't just "raise themselves" – this book is a godsend! Sue's tips really work, and the proof is in the results: her five children are caring, responsible, creative, well-mannered, and just plain FUN to be around. "It takes a village to raise a child," and anyone who works with children can benefit from the support this book provides. Sue, you are awesome!

Annie Smith, B. Ed.
devoted fan, parent of 2

Spend some time with the Kruszewski children and you'll want to know how Sue and Les have raised such an incredible family. Parenting is challenging at the best of times and totally overwhelming at others, but the Kruszewski children are testimony to the fact that Sue knows what she is talking about. If your goal is to raise responsible, caring, thoughtful children who are strong in character, full of spirit, ready to make a difference in this world, and delightful to be with, then you'll want to read Sue's tips on parenting.

Jackie Nicol, B. Ed.
parent of 2

My friend Kim and I were out with our kids. We both have two boys, aged three and five. They were being typical boys – high energy with a great desire to have fun. We started discussing the topic of raising kids and we spoke of how difficult it was to raise amazing kids. Both society and ourselves have such high expectations. I told Kim of my friend Sue, who has five children, every one of whom I would consider amazing. I have known Sue for several years and have often questioned her about how she raised such wonderful kids. She usually says she doesn't know and that she thinks it is just good luck. I don't believe it – I have seen her interact with her kids and watched and learned from her techniques. I am so excited to learn Sue's secrets and be able to incorporate them into my own life as a parent.

Barb Neufeld, R.N., B.Sc.N.
parent of 2 boys

Imagine walking into a house with five small children and everyone is content and quiet. Think I'm making this up? Then you haven't met the Kruszewski family. It is a real pleasure for me to spend time with the Kruszewski kids as they are loving, polite, engaged, kind, and a lot of fun. Sue clearly has a vision for what is possible, and she has made that a reality in her family. The tips she shares in this book will help you do the same. As a new parent, I am really thankful to have this information available to me.

Silvia Marchesin
new mom

Sue has a gift. She empowers her children, celebrates their individuality, and encourages them to love themselves and others for who they are. Together she and Les have created a home that instills confidence and fosters respect. I've always wished that they could bottle their secret so I could use it in my home and in my classroom. Sue has done better. Now with her book, many of us will have the tools, at our fingertips, to support the most important people in our lives, our children.

Nella Bruni, B.Ed
and parent

Sue is not only my sister, but also my idol! I have always looked up to Sue for the amazing job she has done raising her five kids. Raising five kids without any parents to help her along the way! Wow, I think we could all use some pointers from this gal. Thanks to Les, her husband, for also contributing to raising these wonderful children. My two boys absolutely love Sue's kids. They are cousins and also friends. They just always have so much fun together! I myself am so proud of each and every one of these kids, and I can honestly call them my friends. We can all learn from Sue about parenting – this I know!

Sandra Sacco
Business Owner and parent

Ever wonder when you are out and about and you see a GREAT family and think "I want that!"

With Sue's book you will find the answers to get you well on your way.

Watching Sue's family grow up in the last 6 years has been a pleasure; I have learned so much from her and the information she has to give comes from within.

Her dedication to children and the success of families is her true calling; we can all learn from her experiences.

Tracy Bentley
working mom

RAISING WELL-BEHAVED KIDS:

42 Tips from Toddler to Teen
That Really Work!   Sue Kruszewski

RAISING WELL–BEHAVED KIDS

42 Tips from Toddler to Teen That Really Work!

My5 Publishing
4703 15A Avenue
Edmonton, Alberta
T6L 6J1

E-mail: sue@stuff4families.com

PRINTED IN CANADA

This book is dedicated to my incredible family without whom I would have nothing to write about, simply put. Les, Daniel, Char, Hannah, Mia and Ellen – each of you in your own special way has helped me see that I do have lots more to give. You've helped me learn and grow and see that my mission now is to make a difference in other families by helping parents as they raise their children. You've loved me through all my ups and downs and I am stronger because of each of you. Thank you for your unconditional love and support.

Forever,
Mom

Acknowledgements

There are so many people to thank in helping me get my words about parenting onto paper. This has been an incredible journey and one that I could not have completed, or even started, without the unfailing support from my dedicated and loving husband, Les. Without you, Les, I am incomplete, so thank you for helping complete me and the many things "I do"! I love you for always.

Thanks to my wonderful children for supporting me in this whole process – from your kind words and support to getting out there and promoting my books and Web site. All five of you are truly the best gifts God has given me. You are all special and unique and your contribution to the planet will not go unnoticed. And an extra thanks to Char for adding her creative touch to this book in her drawings for Tips 13 and 24. I love it, Char!

To my wonderful sister Sandra, for continuing to help me believe that I can do anything and that one day everything will be worth it. Your support has been immense.

To my best friend, Sil, for your constant encouragement and steady support, not only for me in all I have done, but also for our family over the years. I am so blessed to have a friend like you.

To Annie, Tracy, Connie, Coreen, for always being enthusiastic about my "next venture"! You've hung around for so long; you've helped me stay rooted and focused and believing.

To the cropping ladies in my life, for listening to all my troubles and successes, and life stories, for years now. Thank you for being there when I wasn't doing that great. Your friendship over the years has been essential to my journey. Thanks for not giving up on me and for cheering me on to write this book! Without your continued confirmation, there wouldn't have been a book from me, so thank you.

To my family for your genuine interest in and support for my new projects and business over the years. Thank you.

Thank you to Jens and Nik for your awesome work on the editing and formatting of my book. You have helped make my ideas sound and look really great. Thank you for your guidance and patience.

And to Kathleen, for being that light and guide that I have been seeking for a very long time. I will forever be grateful.

Sue

Acknowledgements

Table of Contents

Introduction

Introduction

Each second we live is a new and unique moment of the universe, a moment that will never be again. And what do we teach our children? We teach them that two and two make four, and that Paris is the capital of France. When will we also teach them what they are? We should say to each of them: Do you know what you are? You are a marvel. You are unique. In all the years that have passed, there has never been another child like you. Your legs, your arms, your clever fingers, the way you move. You may become a Shakespeare, a Michelangelo, a Beethoven. You have the capacity for anything. Yes, you are a marvel. And when you grow up, can you then harm another who is, like you, a marvel? You must work, we must all work, to make the world worthy of its children.

Pablo Picasso

This is one of my absolutely favourite quotations. Raising children in today's world is more challenging than ever before and we must all work to make the world worthy of its children.

As parents, this is one of our responsibilities. Parenting is a full-time job that requires time, commitment, patience, and a hundred more traits than one ever imagined one had. I know this because, along with my dedicated husband, I am raising five children. They range in ages from 9 to 17, one boy and four girls. And, it is a huge job.

My husband and I decided that one of us should be at home for our children. So, after a lot of thought and many dilemmas, I gave up my full-time teaching job and income to be home with our children. And all I can say is that it has been worth every penny and every moment.

I've put together some tips for you in this book that I've found useful along the way, as a parent of kids in school, as a home-schooling parent, as a mom, and as an elementary school teacher and tutor. I hope you find at least a few of them helpful as you raise your own kids, or work with children in general. They are in no particular order of importance – just a collection of tips that we know work.

May you find something that can help you as you travel along on that most incredible journey – parenting, and may you find a few tidbits that you can implement and incorporate into your family's life, starting today.

Tip 1
Laugh Together

Laughter is the shortest distance between two people.

Victor Borge

Tell each other jokes and have fun together. Time spent laughing is always a time that is remembered. When you can make each other laugh, you'll enjoy your time together more. We often tell jokes, watch funny movies or shows together, and share funny stories with each other, and those have been some of the best memories and greatest times.

Visit your local library or school library for joke books and check them out regularly. Have the kids read jokes out loud to you and to each other. Can you come up with some new knock-knock jokes? Those are lots of fun, and there is a never-ending supply of them. Writing them together is a lot of fun, too.

Remember to use sarcasm very carefully and minimally because it can send an underlying message that's different from just plain humour and simple fun.

Tip 2
Be Respectful

When you show your child respect first, your child will respect you in return. Respect is a funny thing. You can't expect to be respected if you first treat a person disrespectfully. It has to be shown first, and then it will be returned to you.

This has been proven to me time and again over the years, in teaching, and at home with my own kids. The principle of respecting first may seem a small thing, but it's enormously powerful. When you have earned the respect of another, a child, you will be able to talk to him and he will listen to you. When I think of this principle, I think of a boy I taught several years ago named Ryan.

Ryan had come to my class from a different school. He had already attended several schools before coming to my school so I knew there was probably a bit of history with this boy. He also came from a single parent family which I gathered might have been difficult for him. When he first walked into my classroom, I knew things were going to be a bit rough at the beginning, but I knew I could be the teacher that could make a difference in this boy's life.

Each morning I greeted him along with my other students at my classroom door with a "Good Morning!" and a short conversation as they entered the room.

Each day I made a point of talking to Ryan, just chatting with him and asking him about different things.

Each day I asked him to be a special helper, do a special job for me, help me out at recess with something fun, etc.

Each day I made sure to state to him directly, out loud in front of someone and anyone, a quality in him that I admired or noticed, or something that he had completed or that he had done well.

And each day, as the year moved on, I saw him get just a little "softer". I saw him grow and become a more confident boy. He could still be a challenge sometimes, but he was nowhere near the closed-off and distant, rough boy that had entered my classroom on that very first day of Grade 4.

At the end of the year, the second last day of school, a few of the students had each brought me a teacher gift. In the small pile was also a gift from Ryan. I opened the others first, purposely saving Ryan's for last. When I opened his gift, I started to cry. In a shabby little box was his absolute favorite NHL pen on a string which he had worn around his neck every day at school, without exception. He was never without it and never let anyone use it, let alone touch it.

I asked if he was sure he wanted to give this to me. He said that yes, he was sure. I put it around my neck as tears filled my eyes. And he said to me: "Mrs. K., you are the best teacher I have ever had."

I was so honoured to have had a chance to make a difference in Ryan's life. I still have that pen as a keep-sake and remembrance of Ryan and to remind me that when respect is first shown to someone else, it often is returned.

Tip 3
Never Finish
Their Sentences

This may sound very funny to you, or maybe you do this and are just realizing now that you do it, but this is a big deal! Never finish sentences for your kids, or for anyone else for that matter. If they are slow to get their words out, be patient and give them the time they need to finish their sentences. Wait for them to finish talking before you add your comments. This shows that you care about them and respect them enough to give them your time to listen to them completely, without interruption or without finishing their thoughts for them.

Tip 4
Get to Know Your Child's Friends and Their Parents

You really get a good idea of what your kids' friends are like by getting to know the parents and the family. You'll learn what values and beliefs they hold and what rules and expectations they have for their children. Even if you do not become the best of friends, make a point of at least meeting the parents and getting to know a bit about them if you can.

You'll be able to tell in a very short time who you do and do not want your kids to spend their time with. When you get to know your children's friends, you also learn about them as individuals, and they may be entirely different from their parents. This is especially true with older teenaged kids.

It has been really neat over the years getting to know our kids' friends and their parents. We have also become good friends with some of the parents, having celebrated many birthday parties and fun times together as our kids have grown up.

Tip 5
Create Realistic
Consequences

There are no long-term or short-term benefits to disciplining your child with a consequence that is unrealistic or irrelevant.

Here are a couple of examples of what may be appropriate and inappropriate consequences:

Cleaning their rooms:

You ask your children to clean their rooms and say: "If you don't clean your room by the end of the day, you will not be allowed to watch TV for a month."

No TV for a month? It might be effective if your children love TV and watch a lot of it, but a month-long consequence for not cleaning their rooms is too long and not appropriate.

A more appropriate consequence might be: "If you don't clean your room by the end of the day, you will be doing your own laundry this week." Or you might say: "If you do not clean your room by the end of the weekend, you will not be having friends over (or not going to a friend's house, possibly) until your room is cleaned."

Clearing their plates from the table:

If your children aren't clearing their plates from the table, and that is something that you would like them to do and learn to make a habit, here's what I've said to my own kids: "I need you to clear your plates from the table, please. If you still have not cleared your plates the third time I ask you, that is the plate you will use for breakfast tomorrow morning. Yes, that is the plate you will use for breakfast tomorrow."

Then, you DO that and follow through with what you said. When breakfast comes the next morning, that's the plate they get to use for breakfast, no choices. That's one way they will learn. You need to keep your word and do what you said you would. We have only ever had to do this ONE time. The kids know that when we ask them to clear their plates, we mean business.

If you break down and give in, and don't follow through on this, all it does is teach them that this really doesn't matter that much, that they don't need to be responsible for their plates, i.e. they don't need to clean up after themselves, and that your word doesn't mean much.

The other thing to remember about creating appropriate consequences is that this technique really works when you are bargaining about something that means a lot to your children. For example, if they absolutely love to play on the hand-held video game, or with a favourite toy, that might be something you take away for a period of time until they complete whatever it is you are asking them to do. Be sure they understand that they will get the item returned to them when they complete the task you requested of them.

Another great example of this is when my husband asks the kids to clear their stuff off the living room floor and return it to their rooms. He puts a large green garbage bag on the floor beside their items and says: "If you do not clear your items off the floor by the end of the day (usually a Saturday), they are going in this garbage bag and will be given away to charity." He has only done this ONCE! The kids know that when Dad says clean up, he means business. Of course, he gives them a couple of warnings to make sure they do what is asked of them.

Tip 6
Be There

Do or do not. There is no try.

Yoda, *The Empire Strikes Back*

Show up. Be there.

It doesn't work to "try" to make it to his game or "just not quite making it" to her dance recital, etc. Of course, there will be times that absolutely won't work out, but I am talking about being there and showing up on a regular, kid-can-count-on-you basis and not saying you'll show up with no intention of following through to be there.

Make a point of taking them out to their sports and extracurricular activities, and watching them when you can. Be involved as the team manager, or volunteer to coach, make phone calls, etc. Keep track of whom they are playing and how they did in the game. Note great plays your child made and plays that weren't so great and talk about these after the game or activity. Recognize their efforts and achievements and tell them you are proud of their efforts. Recognize their growth, rather than whether they won or lost the game. Recognize their hard work, their determination to participate, the great effort they put forth, or their ability as a great team player.

Your children will remember that you were there for them, and they will thank you, maybe not immediately, or maybe not for a long time, but it will have made a difference to them.

If you can, be home or available for them, especially when they are going to encounter something new, like starting junior high.

This year, my kids started Grades 4, 5, 7, 10 and 11. Knowing my third child, I thought she might have some challenges as she started junior high since it would be a big change for her. She's a timid, quiet, easy-going girl who is very thorough and methodical about things.

The night before the first day of school, we got everything ready to go! We got the lunches prepared, all the required supplies organized and ready, and the clothes picked out. She was a bit nervous, but I told her it would be fine. I told her that there would be some things to learn and to adjust to, and it would take some time, but that I knew she could handle it. I told her to take it easy, try to manage things, and to take one thing at a time. I told her to listen carefully to her teachers and just do the best she could. I knew she would do all those things, but I didn't expect what happened when I picked her up after school.

She was the first kid out of the building. Immediately I thought ... hmmmm ... that's odd ... She walked straight to the van and sat in the front seat.

I smiled and said, "How was your first day?"

She simply replied "I am exhausted" and started crying.

Well, it was hard not to cry along with her, without even knowing what had gone on that day. I asked her what had happened in her day and how it had gone. She cried and told me she hadn't felt organized at all, hadn't known where her classes were, hadn't got to eat much of her lunch, and hadn't had a chance to go to the bathroom at all the whole day!

I was shocked and sad. Still trying not to cry, I hugged her and said, "Well, let's look at this and see how we can make things work so that you have a better day tomorrow."

My heart broke for her, but I knew that it would do her no good for me to be a weepy mess! And, I also honoured her and respected myself by allowing her to feel her feelings, without comments or expressing my own feelings. I just allowed her to feel her feelings. Period.

So, we spent the evening talking about her classes, her books, her binder (organizing it in a way that would work for her), and about her teacher's expectations. We looked at and talked about her schedule, when she had her breaks and how to work a bathroom break into her day. We covered all the details we could and then everything else!

By the end of the evening she had calmed down and felt she had a "plan" to work with to help her. She felt more confident about being able to manage and deal with things the next day. At bedtime, I gave her another hug and told her she'd be fine. I told her that this was a new part of her journey in life, a time of transition and learning. I told her too that she was smart enough to be able to handle it all. She again hugged and thanked me for being there to pick her up after school and for helping her out all night. I told her there was no other place I'd rather be.

It was important that I was there for her right after school. I cannot tell you how much of a difference I know it made for her. For the rest of the evening, she kept giving me hugs and each time thanking me for helping her out that day. I still get tears in my eyes thinking about it. It was hard for me to let her go and experience the things I knew she would have to as she learned how to cope. It was worth every moment to be there to "pick her up, dust her off", support her, to be there for her and gently encourage her on to face another day.

Tip 7
Be Involved and Active

Get your hair wet!

Be the parent who takes them swimming, gets in the water to play with them and gets his or her hair wet! Get your hair wet!! This is what your child will remember – not that you drove them to swimming lessons and dropped them off, but that you went into the water with them and hung out with them.

Take them to the park and play with them. Kick the soccer ball around, be the goalie – you get the picture. Not only will they remember that you were involved with them, it will also give you an opportunity to stay active, have fun with your children, and find out about what is going on with them.

Tip 8
Be Patient

Never think that God's delays are God's denials.
Hold on; hold fast; hold out. Patience is genius.

Comte de Buffon

Bite your tongue and give your children a chance to give things a real try without your getting involved. Let them know you are there just by your presence and not by your words. Smile as they try to tie their shoelaces, pour their own juice, cut their own meat, help you put away the groceries, etc. Let them be independent and do things for themselves without your interruption, unless they are tackling a task that is obviously too large or too difficult, or if they are asking for your assistance.

Ask them to do a job and sit back and appreciate they are doing it, without your doing it for them or telling them how to do it, or telling them that they are doing it wrong. Who cares if the shoelace is in a big knot?

Does it really matter if they dented the car as they were learning to drive? Does is really make a difference if the groceries are in the "wrong" place??

In the bigger picture of life, these things won't have mattered. But, it will have mattered that you were there, encouraging them patiently, rather than instructing them or rushing them or criticizing them that it wasn't "done right".

They can be so proud they tied their shoelaces themselves or drove the car to the mall on their own, or helped you put the groceries away. When they do it themselves, give them positive reinforcement and feedback like "Way to go, Mia!" or "Super job doing that yourself, Ellen!" or "WOW! What an amazing job you did, Char!". Cheer them on and encourage them to do more for themselves. This will build respect for you as their parent for your encouragement, and will build their self-confidence as well.

Tip 9
Keep Your Mouth Shut

Before you speak, ask yourself, is it kind, is it necessary, is it true, does it improve on the silence?

Sai Baba

Isn't that a wonderful quotation? It's another one of my favourites! Does it ever say a lot.

Sometimes the best way to teach your children something is to be quiet and let them figure things out for themselves. I think we often give our kids too many instructions or directions and don't let them think for themselves, or find their own answers.

Sit back and be an observer. Watch your children, and before you open your mouth, make a gesture, or jump in to help, ask yourself this question: Do they really need me to comment or assist them at this moment?

If the answer is yes, by all means, help them. If the answer is no, then simply be an observer. Smile. Watch. You will be amazed at what they can do when you let them.

Tip 10
Show Courtesy

Ask your kids to come to the table or take out the trash; don't bark orders. Say please and thank you. Respect their privacy and dignity. Do not rummage through their rooms when they are not home. Do not embarrass them in public, but instead take them aside for correction. Open doors for each other. Let them pass in front of you. Let them "go first". You get the picture ...

Tip 11
Follow the Golden Rule

Teach your children the Golden Rule and follow it yourself: Treat Others As You Would Want to be Treated. This works famously well.

Think about how you treat others and ask whether that is the way in which you would want to be treated: it can really be an eye-opener. Are you treating your children respectfully, kindly, compassionately? If not, then you may have some areas to work on. We all do as parents. None of us are perfect and there will always be areas we need to work on and improve ourselves in.

Use the Golden Rule to assess and determine how you can be a better parent and a better person. It's really a simple tool that helps you see what you are doing well and where you can improve.

And then, turn around and teach your children to use this tool in the same way too. Gently ask them or remind them: "Are you treating that person in a way that you would like to be treated?" or "Is that something that you would like done to you?" They can start using this technique for themselves too, and it will become a habit over time. This technique alone is very powerful and can be life-changing.

Tip 12
Be Present

Love the moment, and the energy of that moment
will spread beyond all boundaries.

Corita Kent

When your child is talking to you, stop what you are doing (preparing supper or whatever), turn around and face them, look at them and listen to what they are saying to you. When you stop what you are doing, it shows them that you care about what they have to say. It also shows them that what they have to say is important enough for you to stop what you are doing and give them your full, undivided attention. This is a huge way to earn your child's respect.

Tip 13
Do Fun Things Together

I am beginning to learn that it is the sweet, simple things of life which are the real ones after all.

Laura Ingalls Wilder

Fun things don't have to cost a lot and they don't need to be really involved or complicated. Keep it simple and just make the time to spend with your children, individually or together as a family. Focus on simply being with them and learning about who they are. You will be hugely rewarded as you become closer to each other.

Here are a few things our family does for fun:

- sledding or skating in the winter
- an annual summer or winter vacation together
- a girls' or boys' night out once a month, or every second week
- a special day with each of the children to do something that he or she enjoys

- a lunch date with one of the children, once a month
- a games night once a week
- a movie night every Friday night
- fun quizzes: favourite colours, favourite food, dislikes, worst fears, happiest moments, favorite teachers and why ...
- silly games and unexpected activities
- swimming at the local swimming pool

This also reminds me of the time when the kids were running around the house (and around the bathroom which has a hallway all around it) into part of the kitchen, then jumping onto the couch in the living room. At first I didn't mind – they were having fun; there was no one working in the kitchen to injure; there were no little toddlers around to run over, and really there wasn't any good reason at the time to stop them.

After a while, I started to get a little annoyed because they were laughing and were getting LOUD – laughing at how high they jumped and from how far they dove onto the couch.

They took a short break and asked if they could have ice cream bars. I said sure – it was a weekend, and everything was all right. Sure enough, within 25 minutes of eating their ice cream bars, the sugar kicked in and they were doing laps around the bathroom and hallway again even faster and louder than before. They would stop at the kitchen, take a bite of their ice cream bars, and then run around again. It really was quite hilarious to watch!

For sure now I couldn't tell them to stop it – they were laughing so much, so high on sugar and running around, jumping on the couch and just sweating ... having the time of their lives. I watched them for a few more minutes and then gave in.

I got up, hid, and waited for them to turn the corner, and then yelled "AAHHHHHHHHHHHH!!!!!!!" and scared the living daylights out of them! It was SO funny. And then, I started doing laps with them!! When they realized I was "chasing" them, they started laughing even more. I followed in their footsteps, and as I came around the corner from the kitchen into the living room, I took a running leap and dove onto the couch!

The kids were totally shocked and immediately started roaring with laughter. When I came around the hallway into the kitchen, I took a bite of someone's ice cream bar, then headed for the living room to take another flying leap onto the couch ... copying exactly what they were doing. They were laughing so hard, I couldn't contain myself either – their laughter was so contagious – we were all just lying on the floor laughing!!

This went on for about another 45 minutes! We had so much fun together that afternoon. They still talk about the time Mom was jumping on the couch!!!!! Of course, it's not something we do on a regular basis and is, in fact, something I discourage, but at this time, it was okay to break the rules to have fun with them, and for Mom to do something completely unexpected!

Tip 14

Be Spontaneous

The soul should always stand ajar,
ready to welcome the ecstatic experience.

Emily Dickinson

This is a great thing to do and similar to tip #13! I love ecstatic experiences!! This shows them that you aren't completely structured and rigid, and that you do like to have fun.

Take them out to a movie on a Friday night, unannounced, or go for a long bike ride on the trails in the river valley. Surprise them with their favourite homemade supper or treat. For example, my kids love bannock. We have an outdoor fireplace and occasionally in the summer we start up the fire pit and have bannock for supper! They love it, especially when it's a surprise. Take them out too for dinner as a special treat every once in a while if you can.

Another great example is the hot air balloon day which they still talk about. A couple of years ago we were driving to the local swimming pool to go swimming. It was a public swim session so we had only a three-hour window of time. We usually go for the whole time because the kids have so much fun swimming and like to be there as long as possible.

On our way to the pool we saw an air balloon almost right above us, and it was coming down!

I said to the kids, "Hey!! Let's go follow it and see if we can see it land!"

They said, "YAAAAAA!"

So we drove around, trying to follow this hot air balloon!

They would yell, "Turn that way!"

"I think it's going over there!", etc.

And I would turn right, then left, following the road to track this air balloon. After about a half-hour of driving, we finally came right up on it!! It was VERY cool.

We came down the winding main road that led us into a new home construction area which took us straight to the hot air balloon! We watched as it came down in a large open lot right between two new houses, right in front of our eyes! We watched as it just cleared the power lines and sank gracefully down to the ground.

The crew of three quickly hopped out of the basket and helped lay the balloon flat as it billowed to the ground. It was so neat to see! We had never seen a hot air balloon that close up – and land right in front of us!! The kids were really amazed and thrilled to have the opportunity to see this marvellous sight.

They were so glad that Mom had been spontaneous and said: "Let's go follow that air balloon and see if we can track it down!" They kept saying, "Thanks, Mom! That was so great!!"

That was an afternoon that they still remember and talk about. And we only missed 45 minutes of the three-hour swim session. What a fantastic, memory-making afternoon that was.

Tip 15
Be Fair

Blessed are the flexible,
for they shall not be bent out of shape.

Anonymous

Treat your children fairly and do not favour one over the other for anything. Don't give in to any outrageous or selfish demands. Keep a backbone so you don't get bent out of shape, but be flexible. I always think of the Golden Rule: Treat Others As You Would Like to be Treated. And that is with respect, fairness and kindness. Treat them all equally and fairly, but be flexible when necessary.

For instance, I tell each one of my kids that he or she is my favourite, but I say it like this: "You are my favourite Miss Mia package!" or "You are my most favourite Ellen package!" It makes them feel special, and I am treating them all the same.

Tip 16
Live Respectfully

Model respectable behavior to help your child learn to act respectfully. Discuss with your child the various behaviors that people can use to demonstrate respect for others. Examples include tone of voice, body language, choice of words, paying attention, saying please and thank you, welcoming people, saying "I'm sorry" and respecting elders.

Try to use these steps when settling disagreements or conflicts to ensure it is done respectfully:

1. Describe what is bothering you using "I" messages.

2. Explain why it bothers you and how you feel about it.

3. Ask your child to explain his or her position.

4. Specify how you want your child to behave, or discuss a solution that is agreeable to both of you.

Remember to think about why your child perhaps isn't sharing your perspective. Really listen and acknowledge what you have heard, and keep in mind that more than one opinion may meet both needs. Approach the resolution in a way that respects your child's perspective and that promotes your child's self-worth.

Tip 17
Let Them Make Mistakes

Don't rescue or save them (unless it's a life or death situation). Let them learn on their own without your input or correction. Let them figure things out for themselves. Often, this is the best way for them to learn something.

Tip 18
Learn to Listen

When people talk, listen completely.
Most people never listen.

Ernest Hemingway

This is one of the most important things you can do for your kids, and perhaps the most important tip in this whole book – learning how to really listen. Learning how to listen effectively is actually a learned skill; did you know that?

My husband and I took a parenting course several years ago, when we just had two little toddlers. It was the best thing we ever did to help us become more effective and better parents. The class taught us many things, but the most important one in my opinion was how to listen. Here's how it works in a nutshell: when your child, for example, gets into an argument with a sibling or friend, and they are really angry, instead of trying to place blame or find out "who did it" or "who started it", the best thing you can do is to simply state to the child what you see:

"I see that you are angry. You and your friend got into a fight (simply stating the facts), and you are really angry (leave out 'about whatever')."

Wait for your child to respond. Don't say anything else. If they still don't say anything, simply repeat your statement:

"You are really angry, I see that. This argument has made you really upset!"

Simply keep restating how your child is feeling. That's it.

Do the same thing when your children come to you crying or upset or angry or experiencing any emotion. It works every time to help diffuse their emotions and calm them down because you are acknowledging them and their feelings. It does not put blame on anyone and simply states the facts. You will be astounded at what happens when you use this amazing technique.

My experience has been that the children stop crying, or calm down, and then either explain what happened and/or then just walk away satisfied that their feelings were acknowledged. Usually, in my experience, children solve their own problems, too. Sometimes they will ask for help and I will offer a few suggestions: you could try this, or try saying that, or what about this? and then let them decide how they best want to handle it.

And, they WILL go on to figure it out themselves, IF you let them. Works like magic.

> *Hearing is one of the body's five senses.*
> *But listening is an art.*
>
> Frank Tyger

Try this "art form", and be consistent. You will truly be in awe of how incredibly well this technique works! You can use this on toddlers and teens and everyone in between!

Tip 19
Acknowledge Feelings

Like in the above tip, acknowledging a person's feelings is extremely powerful, and often this is the only tool needed to help diffuse a situation. When feelings are recognized and simply stated, often that is all that is required to mend things.

And, no one makes you feel anything except you. You have the power to choose whatever feeling you want (see previous point too). You really do! Share this powerful tool with your kids. Tell them that they ALWAYS have the opportunity to choose how they are feeling about a situation. ALWAYS. No one ever tells you how you are supposed to feel. You choose! Neat, eh?

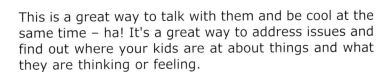

Tip 20
Send Your Kids E-mail!

This is a great way to talk with them and be cool at the same time – ha! It's a great way to address issues and find out where your kids are at about things and what they are thinking or feeling.

My fourth child, Mia, did this with me. She was nine at the time. She sent me an e-mail from the kids' computer downstairs with the subject line "piano issues". I smiled when I saw her message in my Inbox. I knew she had not been happy taking piano lessons, and this was a great way for her to communicate this to me and for me to respond to her.

This is what we wrote:

On May 30, 2007, at 9:16 PM, M K wrote:

mummy i dont like practicing and im not interested in piano.
i also cant learn it very well... i dont like it.sory i didnt tell you before.

Sue Kruszewski <cmsue@shaw.ca> wrote:

Miss Mia – no problem. I have already talked to Paulette to let her know that you and Hannah and Char will not be taking lessons next year! (Ellen would still like to continue.) So, no worries! No worries at all, Miss Mia! I've known that for a while and thought that might be best, to end them for now. You have had three years of lessons so that's all right.
Thanks for telling me :-) Please know you can tell me or ask me anything, any time!
So, you have only one lesson left, and the recital, and then you are done.
I love you,
Mom

PS - I think you CAN learn it just fine, if you wanted to. You can do ANYTHING!

On May 31, 2007, at 10:20 AM, M K wrote:

O.K hannah and i where talking about the piano and i told her to send you a message too.
(i didnt know charlotte didnt like piano)

i love you too.
love: mia

It was a wonderful way for her to communicate her feelings about taking piano lessons. I'm glad she used the computer to talk to me and tell me.

Tip 21
Go For a Drive

I didn't know how valuable a tool this was until I had teenagers and stumbled across this quite by chance. It is another fantastic way to get them to talk to you. If they are big enough, have them sit in the front seat. I've done this with my kids several times, especially the older ones since I first discovered how great this works.

One afternoon, I had some errands to do and needed to drop my son Daniel off at a friend's party on the way. We were in the van for about three quarters of an hour and had a really good chat. He was in Grade 9 at the time and was telling me about the people in his class, and in his grade, and about his friends and about the girl he was going out with! I was surprised. I knew he had a couple of friends who were girls, but I didn't know that he was "officially" dating someone. I wasn't really alarmed or shocked or angry ... just more matter-of-fact-like in my response to him.

Our conversation went like this:

I said, "Oh, how long have you guys been going out?"

He said, "Only a few weeks. We've met up at the movies and gone together with a bunch of friends to see a movie together."

I replied, "Ohhh. I knew you were going to the movies with your friends, but I didn't realize that you and Jackie were going out."

He said, " Yeah ... "

I asked him, "So?"

He said, "So 'What'?"

I asked, "So, do you like her?"

"Yeah, she's all right."

I said, "Just all right?"

"Yeah, she's nice enough. I probably won't go out with her after school's out. I'll probably never marry her."

Smiling, I said, "Really? Then why are you going out with her?"

He said, "Well, if I never went out with anyone, how would I know who is the right girl for me?"

I smiled and said, "Yeah, there's a point there. I can accept that."

Then, SMILING, he said, "You should also know that I kissed her a couple of times."

I said, "Really? How was that for you?"

He looked at me (I think he was shocked at my reply) and said, smiling, "It was really nice."

"Well, good for you. And it is a great thing when you are with a great person. So, what are you going to tell her?"

He said, "Probably just that we are still young and there's lots of time to meet someone, and I know we both want to have a fun summer and not be tied down to anyone."

I said, "Well, that would be a good thing, if that's what you think you need to do."

He said, "Yeah ... it is."

That was one of the best conversations (ha!) we had together, and I knew after that, without a doubt, that we could talk about anything. And he has since approached both my husband and me about questions on different topics.

Tip 22
Expect the Best From Them

Children are likely to live up to what you believe of them.

Lady Bird Johnson

Don't settle for second-rate – in behaviour, in schooling, in anything. When you expect them to do well, and let them know this, they usually meet your expectations. What I mean by this is not to push them or say to them that they had "better get honours in school or else" or "you can be the captain of the team; just get out there and work harder."

Instead, say to them, "I know you are a smart/sharp/bright girl. I KNOW in my heart you can do and be anything you want! There is nothing that is impossible for you."

When you tell them this over and over, from the bottom of your heart, and mean it sincerely, they get that! And that is what they will do. If you haven't started doing this from the time they were little, please start now. You never know where those words will take them, and you will never know how much of an impact those words will make in their lives. When you mean it sincerely, and truly believe they can do or be anything, they will.

Be positive and supportive. Of course, the principle of reinforcement will operate just as effectively in the negative way. If you continually tell them that they are stupid or useless, that is also what they will believe and become.

So be sure to reinforce in their minds NOW, even if you haven't done this before now, that they are bright, talented, smart, beautiful, special, kind, whatever. Do this REGULARLY and start NOW. This is something that will impact their lives enormously.

Tip 23

Teach Good Manners & Model Good Manners

*Manners are a sensitive awareness
of the feelings of others.
If you have that awareness,
you have good manners,
no matter what fork you use.*

Emily Post

Expect them to do the same and be consistent.

I grew up in a home where manners were VERY important. My parents always made sure we said please and thank you when we asked for something or received anything. We called adults by their title of Mr. or Mrs. We asked permission to leave the table, or to enter a family's home. We were never allowed to barge in, help ourselves to anything without asking first, or to walk away without an acknowledging thank you when given something. Although it wasn't extreme, my parents were thorough and consistent. It was always the same – their expectation of exceptional manners. This was the one thing I vowed to do with my own children.

Make sure your children know the correct way to behave in public and understand the rules. For example, teach them how to make introductions and rehearse good table manners with them. Familiarity breeds success.

As a parent, we want our kids to shine when they interact with others. Here are 10 of the most important manners to teach your kids:

1. Always say please, thank you, and excuse me.
2. Send thank-you notes for gifts: with a note card, a phone call or an e-mail.
3. Look people in the eyes when speaking to them.
4. Pick up clothes left on the floor; put dirty dishes in the dishwasher.
5. Wait your turn to speak and do not interrupt.
6. Have good phone manners and take good phone messages.
7. Be thoughtful and considerate of others – especially about opening doors and offering seats to older people.
8. Listen when others speak and respond clearly when spoken to.
9. Respect the privacy and property of others.
10. Use proper table manners (see below).

None of these are impossible to achieve and all are traits and practices that will serve your children well in their future too. With consistency, persistence and role modelling, your kids will make you and themselves proud!

Eight Steps to Good Table Manners

Whether it's dinner at a friend's house or a formal meal, most of us judge people based on their table manners. But what can you do if your kids are burping and slurping their way through dinner?

Here are steps to set your child on the road to good etiquette:

1. Look for the good. Instead of pointing out the things that your child does wrong, point out what she or he does right. Say, "I was so proud of you when we went to Tracy and Andrew's for supper. It was wonderful the way you helped yourself when the appetizers were served."

2. Don't turn dinner into an unpleasant "lecture time". That will turn kids off not only to manners, but to dinner, and to you, too.

3. Check your own example. Don't show up for dinner in your underwear unless you want your kids to do the same.

4. Don't label your child as a slob. Instead, point out the behaviour in a neutral, practical way. For

example, say: "It's a good idea to unfold your napkin so if food falls, you won't stain your clothes."

5. Approach manners as a game. One night each month or so, try to have a somewhat more formal dinner. Try dressing up, serve a special meal, and expect more formal manners. That will help improve your kids' social graces.

6. If (or how about "when"!) you hear a burp, explain that in some cultures burping is a way of showing one's appreciation, but here in North America it's considered rude. If you were to do that in someone else's house, he or she might think you're a slob and may not want you to come back.

7. Make kids part of the tradition. Invite guests over and let kids help serve appetizers. This helps them indirectly learn about the manners that surround eating.

8. Try dining out once in a while. Fast-food restaurants don't count; dining over Styrofoam doesn't bring out the best in manners. And you can't pull someone's chair out for her if it's bolted to the floor. Try a nice restaurant and allow kids to order their own food, and to assist in figuring out the tip.

And don't lose heart (or your cookies) if your kids' manners at home are atrocious. Often these same kids exhibit outstanding behaviour outside the home when you are not there. If you're getting positive reports from other people outside the home, that's great. You can trust that your kids are learning a few things and are developing great manners.

Tip 24
Be a Great Role Model

Did you know that your actions speak louder than your words?

I'm sure you knew this, and I know this is a cliché, but it's so true! I can't tell you how many times I've seen the same behaviours from my children as ones that I exhibit myself, good and not-so-good! It's amazing!

When you SHOW them how to behave, what to do in situations, how to respond, how to act, eventually they turn around and do the very same thing as you have shown them. Often, we don't even see this in ourselves, but it's there – if you just observe your children. It's amazing. (Did I already say that? Ha!)

You can tell them to be a nonsmoker when they grow up but chances are good that if you are a smoker yourself, that's what they will be as well. The same goes for use of language. If you often use colourful language, there's a good chance your children will too. Attitudes? Same thing. If you consistently make comments about a certain group of people, it's likely that your child will reflect the same. What about eating over the sink? Dirty socks on the floor? Not clearing your plate from the table after a meal? Rude comments at atrocious drivers?? You get the picture.

Watch what you say and how YOU behave. Often, that is the biggest factor in determining whether you raise a well-behaved child or one that isn't so well-behaved.

It reminds me of a story a friend of mine told me about her three-year-old boy. She was in the kitchen and he was in the living room playing with his blocks. He got into building a tower with his blocks but after a few minutes, his wonderful tower came crashing down. He was so upset, he yelled out loud, "Oh shit!" His mom, my friend, started laughing to herself, but at the same time was so shocked at the word that had come out of his mouth. Of course, she talked to him about using "good" words and "bad" words and not using swear words.

When her husband came home that night, she told him about their son and the blocks and the "s" word that their child had said. Her husband looked at her and said, "Well, you know where he gets that from, don't you?" ... long pause ... "You!!," he said.

She was speechless. She had not realized before how often she had said that particular word in earshot of their son. Anyway, it was an eye-opener for her, no question.

Tip 25

"I Love You"
or a Hug, or BOTH!

What can you do to promote world peace?
Go home and love your family.

Mother Teresa

Be sure to either TELL your kids you LOVE them or give them a hug, or do both! This is an amazing tool that requires very little from you, except to be genuine, and it does miraculous things for your child. And, your teens need this more than you think they do!! I still give my teenaged kids a big fat hug or I tell them out loud that I love them (and often in front of other people too – ha). It's very neat seeing their reactions.

It's best to start this, of course, right from the beginning when your kids are tiny, and to be consistent. They need to hear it in your words and feel it in your touch. They need this more than you think, and, in my opinion, there can never be enough hugs and I Love Yous.

The best thing about this are the reactions you will get. I remember talking to my son after school one day and he was in a foul mood. I asked him a few times what was wrong and whether I could do anything to help. He just grumbled and didn't make much eye contact with me.

So, I went right up to him as he sat in his chair at his computer, gave him a big fat hug, kissed him on the cheek and told him I loved him no matter what. It was a pure, priceless moment that turned his whole demeanour around! He blushed a little and gave me a big hug. With a smile on his face, he said to me, "I love you too, Mom. And thanks."

That moment was worth a million bucks.

That moment also confirmed for me once again that teens need to hear it just as much as the littler kids. So DO that. It IS worth a million bucks to your child, too.

And waiting for the "right moment"? There may never be one, and time passes way too quickly for those I Love Yous and hugs to not be given.

Tip 26
Never Assume

Do you know what assume means?

It has been described to me like this:

Never *assume* because it makes an *ass* out of *u* and *me*! The first time I heard this I thought, "WOW. That makes a lot of sense." From that moment on, every time I hear the word assume, the idea of being an ass by assuming to know what people think, feel, want, etc. immediately comes to mind.

I've tried consistently to bear this in mind whenever I meet people, and it really is a great tool. You may think you know how someone is feeling, or what they are thinking, or what they are going through, but it can never be confirmed or dismissed until you get the actual story from the person ... straight from the horse's mouth. Only then can you decide whether your assumptions are correct.

This is so true for kids, and such a great tool to use with them. Let them tell you what happened, what they are thinking about, or how they are feeling. Do this before you decide yourself what you think happened, or what you think they are thinking, or what you think they are feeling. When you check in with them first, putting all assumptions aside, and let them express their thoughts, feelings and words to you, you will be surprised at the times you may be wrong! At least, that has been true for me.

So encourage them to talk, to tell you what is happening to them, without your making any assumptions about them or the situation. Keep from making an ass of yourself or of them. This REALLY works, and it is pretty cool.

Parenting IS
Top Priority

Make rules and be sure to enforce them. Children WANT rules set out by their parents even though they may never say so, or may say the opposite. It shows them you care about what happens to them. Adapt the rules as needed as your child gets older and more independent.

Know that this unpaid and often unrecognized job of parenting is THE most important job you will ever have. Truly it is, because you have the power to make a difference for the next generation. You have the power to influence the future in enormous ways. And you have to always keep that in the forefront of your mind, always. This is the most influential job you could ever have, simply because of the impact it has on the future, your children's future.

And because of this simple fact alone, it is your job to never give up! It comes in the unwritten job description

– you are not allowed to give up. At any moment and at any time, you are not allowed to give up. You have to believe that this work of parenting, every moment, every interaction, is significant in shaping your child who is the future. And it IS!

You will at times feel like quitting, like giving up, like saying "What's the point, anyway?" or "It won't matter, anyway", etc. But, it does matter!! I've seen it in my own kids. You cannot give up. You have to keep going.

And for those times when you do feel like giving up or quitting, have someone to call for support – your spouse, a family member, a friend, a support network, someone. If you don't have someone out there for you, FIND someone TODAY. This is essential. We all need support, no matter how good we think we are or how much we think we can handle. There will come a time when you will need help, so do not be afraid to ask, or feel inadequate. ASK for help and support. This is worth a mint and will help you keep focused on your parenting job as top priority.

On top of all of this, it is not about you. It's about your children and doing what is best for them, keeping in mind you have to nurture and feed yourself too in the process of nurturing and feeding them.

Tip 28
Every Child is Different

If you can't feed a hundred people, then feed just one.

Mother Teresa

Every child is different and what works with one may not work with another. Sometimes, it's a matter of trial and error and just seeing what works with each of your children. So "feed" one at a time, and make a huge impact on that one, and then the next, and the next, and soon you will be doing the "impossible".

Start by doing what's necessary, then what's possible, and suddenly you are doing the impossible.

Saint Francis

Our third daughter is the perfect example. She and my husband would often butt heads. He would ask her to do something; she wouldn't do it. He would ask her again, raising his voice to her, and she would become even more stubborn. Finally, he'd be yelling at her, at which point she would become really defiant. Often, the interactions he had with her were negative ones.

I looked at this situation and wondered why my own interactions with her were so different. I realized that it was because I had spent much more time with her, being the stay-home parent and having learned effective ways of dealing with her. I dealt with her in a different manner. Instead of raising my voice, I spoke quietly to her, face to face at her level. I suggested to him that instead of yelling at her, he go close to her and look her in the eyes, putting an arm around her and in a quiet voice asking her to do what it was that he wanted her to do.

He tried this and got an amazing first-time result with her! He was so surprised. He's done that ever since with her, and it works like a charm. I figured out that Hannah doesn't like yelling and doesn't respond at all to requests in that manner (who does really, anyway!). It was a learning experience for both of us, no question.

I've realized over the years that every child is different and reacts differently to things. Raising children calls for and requires different techniques, most of which are often learned by trial and error, in my experience.

Tip 29
Pick Your Battles

This applies to toddlers and to teens. Does it really matter if the clothes your child has chosen for the day do not match? Does it really matter that her hair is not in a perfect ponytail, or that his socks don't match?

No. It doesn't matter. It really doesn't!

What matters is how proud they feel when they can say they picked their clothes themselves, got dressed themselves, did their hair on their own or washed their hair themselves.

And does it really matter that your teen's room is messy? I guess it could make a difference if it became a dangerous place to walk into, or small rodents were breeding in a corner of the closet. If your teen is doing well in school, has good friends, has interests or hobbies, and isn't into anything questionable or unsafe, then does it really matter that his or her room is a mess? I know this might be a point of disagreement, but I think if my teen is on track, doing all right, I can handle a messy room. That's just my opinion and is something to think about ...

Tip 30
Give Them Choices

This is a great technique that works with kids of all ages. If an issue or argument is brewing, for example, about the children not wanting to eat their green beans, offer them a choice. Say, for example, "You can eat all of the beans on your plate, or two beans and some carrots from the fridge."

Usually when you offer them a choice, it gives them some freedom and leeway and ends the escalation of a situation. Preventing a situation from escalating is obviously the best thing to do. And really, so what if all he eats are two beans and some carrots? I'm just happy he's eating SOME veggies!

Same thing would go for clothes. If your child wants to choose her clothes to wear for the day, and you want her to wear specific items, offer her a couple of outfits to choose from. For example, say, "You can wear either this outfit or this outfit." Usually that works, but if it doesn't, does it really matter? That's something I guess you have to decide. To me, if she's dressed and clean and happy, and we are out the door on time, great! I have also explained to her why certain clothing choices/colours don't work together. This helps her learn to make more knowledgeable choices on her own.

Another great example of this occurred with my nephew just recently. It was late morning and my sister came by with her little guy while doing her errands. She stopped in, we had coffee, and then I started to prepare lunch for all of us. She was glad about that because he was getting a bit cranky and restless. I got together some leftover pasta salad and veggies. She was in a bit of a hurry, with errands to do, and so had to rush through lunch a bit.

Well, Evan, being two and a half, cannot be rushed. We sat down and he looked at his bowl, tasted the noodles and said, "These are cold." He asked me to warm them up. We had a discussion about the noodles being cold because it was a pasta salad. He wasn't quite getting it because he had always known noodles to be warm and not cold, as in a pasta salad.

My sister started getting annoyed with him and said, "No. You'll eat them cold because we have to go." He was getting upset because he wanted them warmed up, and she was getting more and more frustrated because he wasn't listening and was insisting on not leaving because his noodles were cold. I asked him if he wanted to eat his noodles warmed up, or if he wanted something else. He said he wanted his noodles warmed up.

So, I told her I'd quickly warm them up and she could load up the truck and be ready to go as soon as he was ready. She agreed and loaded up things while I "heated up" his pasta salad in the microwave! I set the thing to low power for just 10 seconds so his pasta salad wasn't cold from the fridge but just barely room temperature.

He was happy that he got his noodles "heated up". I told him to take the coloured bowl which he had picked from the drawer for his noodles (again, his choice from the drawer of plastic dishes) and a special spoon, and he could eat the noodles in the truck because Mommy was in a hurry to get going. He happily toddled off with his bowl of "heated-up noodles" and special spoon in hand. My sister just shook her head and smiled.

By simply taking a moment to make things a bit lighter, situations that are escalating, such as this one with my nephew, can be diverted and have a happy ending.

Tip 31
In Whose Best Interest?

Sometimes this is a hard one to decipher, but a great question to ask yourself: Is this in my child's best interest or in mine? And you can also ask yourself: Do they need to be "saved" or do they need to experience this themselves? Most of the time, they need to experience things for themselves.

A great example of this occurred recently when one of my daughters had a bit of a conflict with her best friend. After lunch one day (this was early-dismissal day so three of my kids were home early), I asked: "So, did anything significant or insignificant happen this morning at school?"

Two of them said no, and then the third said yes. So I asked her what happened. She started telling me the whole story. She and this girl have been best friends since kindergarten. As she was telling me the events that happened, she started crying. (Again, it was hard for me not to cry along with her!!!)

As she was telling me the whole story, I really felt angry that her little friend hadn't given her a chance to explain herself. Part of me wanted to pick up the phone and call the mom and tell her to talk to her kid! Of course, I had to remind myself that I didn't know the whole story or all of the events that had happened between the two girls. I also had to remind myself that it really was not my problem, and that Hannah needed to figure this out and deal with it on her own. I would support her, but she was the one that needed to pick up the phone, as I had suggested to her, and call her friend to explain, apologize or sort this out.

It may have been in my best interest to call up this mother and talk to her about the situation myself, but it was in Hannah's best interest to deal with this situation directly and on her own, without my involvement, and to come to a resolution herself.

And she did that. She called her friend three times and finally got the chance to talk with her directly. Later on, I asked her how it had gone with her friend and she said, "Everything's great!" I'm so glad I stepped back and let her figure it out for herself. I know she learned a lot because of this event.

Tip 32
Call Your Kids Names!

Ha! I mean, don't call them bad names, but call them fun names. Do they have a nickname? If not, make one up that suits them and use that as your special name for them. Do they have a name that they like to be called? If so, use that one too. For example, I often call my kids Sweetie. I know they like it when I call them that. They just smile, or blush ... but it makes them feel good, makes them feel special.

Other fun names I've called them include Sweetie Pie, Handsome (for my son and sometimes to be funny, for my daughters, too!), Beautiful, Gorgeous, Cutie, Sweetie. I call my fourth child "Miss Mia" as that just seems to fit her pretty well.

Stay away from calling them words with connotations or meanings that aren't so positive. For example, chubby, tubby, poopsie, poopy and midget, and anything that could be derogatory, are good ones to stay away from.

You can have lots of fun with this but just remember to remain respectful, and be sure it's a name that your child likes to be called and that's it's positive.

Tip 33
Pray Every Day

*Prayer is not asking for what you think you want,
but asking to be changed in ways you can't imagine.*

Kathleen Norris

Believe that there is some higher power, whatever you want to call it … something bigger, beyond you and your current reality, that is listening and does hear you. It doesn't have to be what we usually understand to be "God". Say a prayer every day, even if only a single line, or something that may seem meaningless, or that comes from rote memory.

The perfect example of the need for prayer occurred when my first three kids were little. They were one-, three-, and four-years old and dependent on me for all their physical and emotional needs. My husband was in university full-time and I was working full-time. Every morning I had to be up at 5:30 a.m. to get myself ready for my teaching job and my kids ready for the day home. Mornings were crazy and included this list of tasks:

- packing up the kids' backpacks
- sending a special lunch for my son (who had food allergies at the time and was on a special diet)
- making sure there were enough diapers and a change of clothes for each child (often I prepared the diaper bag and lunches the night before)
- packing up my marking, papers, school books and my own lunch
- packing my husband's lunch
- making breakfast and feeding the kids, and myself
- washing up, brushing teeth, getting dressed and getting the kids dressed
- loading up the car with everything to drop the kids off at the day home by 7 a.m. and being at work by 8 a.m. (I had a one-hour commute each way)

There were days when all I could say was: "Lord, help me survive today." And that is ALL I could say each day, for many months. My plate was more than full, and on top of it all, I was dealing with an ailing father and still grieving over the loss of my mom.

Every morning when that alarm clock rang at 5:30 a.m., I silently prayed: "Lord, help me through this day."

And, I know now, for a fact, that that simple prayer helped keep me going, and grounded, and helped me literally survive until there was a time I could do more.

So, pray every day, whatever that means for you – even a single line – because you don't realize just how much of an impact that will have on your life down the road. You may not see immediate help or results, but I can tell you without question, that it does really make a difference. And, when you are being supported, you will in turn be able to support and guide your children and family better, too.

And ...

> *If the only prayer you ever say in your entire life is thank you, it will be enough.*

Meister Eckhart

Tip 34
Give Them Tools

Teach them the strategies they will need in order to survive and cope with the big and small changes in their lives ... changes like starting a new grade, starting junior high or high school, moving to a new school, or having a teacher that they don't get along with very well.

Give them specific strategies and guidelines on how to deal with these challenges and provide alternative suggestions and options.

I remember, for example, when my oldest was starting high school. I asked him what he needed to assist him in the change to a new school. I asked him whether he wanted me to come to the school with him to register or whether he wanted to do it by himself. He thought about this for a day or two and then told me he wanted to go in himself.

If your child doesn't know what might help them, then offer specific tools and strategies.

Give them a fork! Hahahaaaa. Really, if they need a fork, give it to them!!!

Seriously though, here are some strategies that have worked for us in raising our own kids.

General Time Management

- Sit down with your children to examine how they spend their time. Include school, sleep, meals, sports practice, homework time, social activities, religious study, etc. Colour in a pie chart or use an hour-by-hour day planner for a visual representation of a typical day.
- Use the chart to identify bottlenecks or overscheduling. To resolve issues, look for chances to reschedule activities at another time or to cut them out.
- Help your children become aware of time and scheduling by pointing out conflicts as they occur. If there's time either to go to the birthday party or to visit with Grandpa, let him or her make the choice when it doesn't involve a must-do situation.
- Post a family calendar in an accessible place. If you have little ones, make sure it's in a place where they can see it at eye level. We have one in our kitchen and one in the office so they're always easy to refer to. Use your calendar to track family commitments and your children's classroom assignments and other activities.
- If you don't have a cordless phone already, get one. That way you can talk and go to the calendar when you need to! These are priceless!!

Weekly Planning

- Set aside a time each weekend, perhaps Saturday morning or Sunday evening, to plan the upcoming week with your child. Also set aside a bit of time for meal planning for the coming week for your family. Make this a habit and it will help make your meal-times easier!
- Make a to-do list, noting when school tasks and household chores must be finished. Crossing off completed items gives your child a sense of accom-plishment. Teach your children how to make to-do lists too.
- Make sure the family calendars are always up-to-date.

The Morning Routine

- Always prepare the night before. Choose clothing, gather books and assignments, and put everything in a specific place.
- Make lunches the night before and have them ready to go in the fridge. Have a bin in the fridge labeled FOR LUNCHES ONLY with snack items. That way, healthy snacks are ready to go and no one has to spend additional time in the morning searching for snacks to put in his or her lunch.
- Set the alarm clock early enough to provide necessary time to get ready. If it's an electric clock, be sure the back-up battery is still good.
- For younger kids, make a list or picture chart of the tasks in the morning routine, such as brushing teeth, eating breakfast, and getting dressed. Have them

mark each task as it's completed. When it becomes habit and routine, checking it off may not be necessary.

- Again for younger kids, post a list or pictures of everything your child should have as he or she walks out the door, such as backpack, jacket, lunch, school papers, homework, etc.
- Be specific when checking whether your kids have remembered everything. Ask "Do you have your science book?" or "Do you have your lunch?" Simply asking if they have "everything" as they rush out the door is not really useful.

Your Child's Room

- Survey your children's rooms from their perspective. Sit in a chair, lie on the bed and see things their way. Talk to them about the space and storage needs for their various supplies, activities, and treasures.
- Organize for each activity, e.g. getting dressed requires a hamper for dirty clothes, reachable closet rods, and dresser drawers with enough space to store things neatly. His school books and supplies will need a bookshelf with bookends. His computer will need a desk that is big enough to hold his monitor, computer, mouse, CDs, etc.
- Use creative storage solutions. Try a door-hung shoe holder for action figures, games, or trading cards. Clay pots or tin cans can be decorated and neatly hold markers, crayons, or paint brushes. A bookshelf can be made using his old skateboard or a couple of shortened hockey sticks. Check out IKEA for tons of cool storage ideas.

- When the room is neat and organized, take photographs of how it looks. Place them in a spot where your child can check frequently to see if his room still matches the pictures.
- Sort through his stuff on a regular basis. Work together to choose outgrown clothes and toys to be discarded or donated. Rearrange his room if it needs a change of layout, or to clean out the dust bunnies! We do this at least twice a year, usually once in the winter and once at the end of the school year, going through all his or her clothes, belongings and room furniture.

Organization for School

- Have a designated place for your child to keep his or her backpack, homework, lunch kit and papers for school. As soon as your child comes home from school, those items need to be put in those designated places.
- Get a sturdy three-ring binder or Duo-Tang with coloured pocket dividers for each subject. Coach your child to slip all assignments into the proper section, and check regularly to see that it's being done. Alternatively, find a method that works for you both if it's not a three-ring binder. Maybe a file folder with only one opened side would work.
- Include a pocket labeled "Home" for anything that needs your attention, if this is not set up already somehow from school.
- Provide a calendar or assignment page for noting homework, tests, projects, etc. Transfer this information to your family calendar. If your children do

have school agendas, make sure they are writing in them at the end of every school day. If they do not have school agendas, get notebooks or scribblers and start them.

- Be sure to talk with their teachers and enlist their help, if needed, to ensure assignments are entered in the agendas consistently and correctly.
- Help your children maintain their binders by going through the papers with them, putting things in order, and discarding unneeded items on a regular, daily or weekly, basis.

Practice Makes Perfect

New habits take time to learn, especially if bad habits need to be unlearned first. Don't give up. Your children may need frequent reminders, lots of help, and consistency. Of course, pitch in; they can benefit from watching you arrange their rooms, finding places for their stuff and putting things in good order. Remember to reward their successes and give them a little extra help when they are feeling discouraged. The strategies you teach them now will pay off for the rest of their lives.

Tip 35

Answer Questions Honestly

Integrity is foundational.

When your children ask you questions about puberty, sex, religion, drugs or any other topic, answer them honestly, with integrity and with compassion. When you tell them your own experiences, it helps them relate to you on a deeper level and also helps build trust. Sharing honestly with them strengthens the bond between you and your children. It lets them know that they can come to you with anything and you will honour and respect them. This is HUGE.

A perfect example of this occurred when one of my daughters was just beginning her periods. One evening she came to me and said: "Mom, I have to talk to you alone in your room." I had a feeling it was about this topic, but I wasn't sure. So, I finished up with my other child and went and met her in my room.

She started telling me about the changes she was noticing in her body, and she started crying. I comforted her and just asked her what was wrong. She said she was nervous about the whole period thing and just didn't know anything. It was hard not to cry along with her (have I said that before! ha) but I reassured her she would be fine.

I told her about my first experience with all this and she listened so intently. It was such a pure and deep moment of sharing and openness with her. After I told her about my own story, she started asking me specific questions about her body, her period, her cycle, feminine protection and everything else that came to mind. We spent two and a half hours that night talking about it all. At the end of it, she said to me, "OK Mom, that's enough. I think I've had all the info I can take for one night." I just laughed!

She left my room feeling confident about how she would handle all of this at school, and with Physical Education and all. She had all her questions at that time answered and felt secure in knowing too that if she needed, she could come to me for more support.

Since that time, she has come to me about other things that she has had questions about and issues she was facing. I cannot tell you how good it feels to know that she trusts me immensely and knows that I will be there for her when she needs me. There was no other place I wanted to be but in that room with my daughter helping her deal with this major change in her life.

Tip 36

Do Not Give Them
Everything They Want

*To be without some of the things you want
is an indispensable part of happiness.*

Bertrand Russell

This is one of my favourite quotations because it simply reminds me that happiness lies not in having "stuff" but in enjoying the things you do have and being appreciative of those things.

As my mom also used to say to us: "To feel rich, count the things that money cannot buy." In fact, she had handwritten this quotation on a piece of notepaper, framed it, and hung it on the wall in our kitchen.

We saw that note and read that message every day. Growing up, I incorporated this message into my life. It is a fundamental value that I have made sure to pass on to my children.

This value quite simply helps prevent kids from becoming spoiled, selfish, misbehaved, demanding and ungrateful – in a nutshell!

Teach them that they need to work for things they want. Teach them the value of work and the value of a dollar. But also expect them to help around the house, do chores and yard work because it needs to be done and they need to contribute, and not for pay.

Do not give them some "thing" as compensation for your lack of discipline, or to make them feel better, or to try to make up for something else that you think is lacking in their lives or for time not spent with them. This is one of the worst things you can do.

Teach them to appreciate what they have and the value of work and effort and most importantly, that having a "thing" or "everything" does not bring happiness.

TO FEEL RICH
COUNT THE
THINGS YOU
HAVE THAT
MONEY CAN'T
BUY .

MOM!

Tip 37
Do Not Compare

*Never look down on anybody
unless you're helping them up.*

Jesse Jackson

Did you ever like being compared to a sibling as you were growing up? Do you like being compared to a sibling or cousin or neighbour, even now as a grown-up?

I'll bet probably not. Each one of us is different and has different talents, abilities, gifts, and skills. And no one should be compared to anyone else.

You might want to talk about how much better your children have done this time on a test or how much better they could do, but not how well they did compared with their friends, or others in the class.

Praise them for their own individual talents and abilities, how they are improving in piano lessons or in Karate, how much further they have come since the beginning of the year or how much better they can perform that skill.

This will do more for their self-esteem and for their respect for you than you could ever imagine.

Tip 38
Be Thankful

Love wholeheartedly, be surprised, give thanks and praise – then you will discover the fullness of your life.

Brother David Steindl-Rast

There are lots of things to be thankful for, and when you think you have no reason to be thankful, force yourself to think of all the benefits you have around you. Recognize all the good things that surround you: things that have come your way, people you have met who have become good friends and anything that has made your day a special one.

Silent gratitude isn't much good to anyone.

Gladys Browyn Stern

Every suppertime that we are together, and when we can, we take turns saying what we are thankful for in our day. Everyone gets a turn, and you can pass if you don't want to say anything. No one else talks until that person is finished saying what he or she is thankful for.

It starts with whoever would like to start and usually goes around the table from person to person. Sometimes, someone will jump in because something "really good" happened that day, and that's fine too.

I start it off by saying, "So, what are you thankful for today, Ellen?" And she'll think of something, say her special something, end it with "Amen", and then it goes around the table. This is a great way to connect as a family, and suppertime I found has been the best time to do this, a time when we are usually together as a family.

Everyone knows to respect each other and listen when someone else is speaking. No one makes fun of or teases anyone or makes comments, unless it's a positive one on what the speaker is thankful for.

Often, the thing they are thankful for becomes a short prayer. For example, often the kids will be thankful for the meal we are sharing. It may be one of their favourite meals and they are enjoying the taste and experience of it. Then we often pray and remember those who don't have hot delicious meals or warm comfortable homes, etc., as we have right now.

It has brought us closer and has taught us to respect one another. Lots of times we laugh and sometimes cry, and end up having other stories to share around whatever it is they mention they are thankful for.

This has been a wonderful tradition for us. I started it with the family when the kids were really little, and it's something now that is really special for all of us.

Tip 39
Never Give Up

Clear your mind of "can't".

Samuel Johnson

When you think that your hard work and attempts to be a good parent are failing, that is the time you must stay the course, be consistent, and NOT GIVE UP! I know this is true for I have experienced it many times in my life as a parent and teacher.

My son, Daniel, who is 17 now, is a perfect illustration of this point.

As Daniel went through his toddler years, he seemed to be okay – well-behaved and well-mannered. He had always been a challenge to keep busy though, as he was a very active child, but he didn't get into much trouble, just the odd fight or disagreement. When Daniel started kindergarten, things changed.

He became more aggressive and even MORE busy and active than he had been at home with me. In his kindergarten year, he was often sent to the principal's office for fighting in class with the other boys. There were a lot of kids in his class that year – 28 to be exact – and on top of that two-thirds of them were boys! My only guess is that this was the year in which he had to figure out how to get along with a whole bunch of other boys!

I really don't know what made him get into the number of fights he did, but I was absolutely horrified each time I got a call from the school about my "certain someone" being in the principal's office that day. This went on throughout kindergarten AND Grade 1, much to my disappointment and concern.

I continued to talk with him each time about his behaviour and the right things to do. I continued discussing the situation with his teacher. I continued to believe in him as a good little person who was just figuring out his way. I had to. I wanted to do all I could to provide the guidance and direction he needed, despite the many times it seemed I wasn't getting through to him!

Can you imagine if I had decided: OK, that's enough! One more call from that school about "that kid" being in that office, and I'm done with him! What would have happened if I had given up on him and not continued being consistent, encouraging and positive? I'm not sure, but things could have significantly deteriorated for him (and me).

And now, do you know what this boy, who was often in the principal's office in kindergarten, is doing? He is a Grade 11 honour student with a fantastic and huge circle of friends. He is a responsible, compassionate, loving, conscientious, confident, morally upright, fun-to-be-around, positive teen whom many kids, especially his younger sisters and cousins, look up to.

And I am so proud to say he is my son.

So, my point is this: you cannot give up, even when it is difficult and challenging. You cannot say, "I can't do this." You HAVE to remain consistent, continuously patient, and always positive. And you HAVE to always BELIEVE that you are making a positive difference in the life of your child.

Clear your mind of "can't". Because you CAN.

Tip 40
Use Discipline Wisely

Discipline in private; praise in public.

I have used this technique over the years as I've raised my kids and taught elementary school. It's a gem, and it is something that REALLY works. It builds respect. You gain your children's respect because it shows that you care and respect your children enough to not embarrass them or make them feel bad about themselves or the situation.

When you see that your children are doing something inappropriate, simply call their names or approach them quietly. Tell them: "I need to see you for a minute" or "(Child's name), come here for a moment". Recap what you saw or what happened or what the situation or event involved. Tell them that you weren't happy when you saw _____ because of _____. Tell them what you saw, why YOU weren't happy, and what YOU would like to see them do differently, and offer a couple of options. Reprimand them respectfully.

Use "I" statements and talk about how "I" feel about this rather than saying "You did this wrong" or "You caused the fight" or "You misbehaved", etc. "I" statements are powerful in that they keep things objective and don't place blame or fault. "I" statements also allow you to express your feelings about the situation. Say, for example, "I am upset about this situation because it makes me feel _____."

Another thing that works superbly well is to talk to them quietly, ESPECIALLY when you are angry or upset about something they have or have not done. Most kids do not respond very well to yelling. True! Believe me, I have had a chance to test this theory out ☺, and I know when I have responded by yelling, it has been usually considerably less effective than the times I have responded in a quiet, controlled manner. Talk quietly and rationally. That is WAY more effective than shouting.

Praise their good work, good deeds, and achievements in front of others, but do not compare. Just simply say, "WOW, Mia! You did great on your math test!" or "That's terrific, Hannah! You did your best on the Social test and you got a great mark!" or "What a wonderful job you did sweeping the floor! Thank you" or "Great job putting the groceries away! Thank you."

Does that make sense? This is HUGE. Whenever possible, use "I" statements, talk to them quietly to correct them and praise them in public for their good works. No one likes being yelled at, or scolded, or talked down to. Don't do that to your child. You will see that they will respect you even more down the road if you use these techniques consistently.

Tip 41
Get Down on Your Knees

Get down to your children's eye level when you are talking to them. Make sure you have their attention and that they are looking right at you when you are speaking to them. Do not start speaking until you have eye contact with them. That way, they know you mean it, and what you say will get through to them. This really works great on everyone but is really effective for smaller kids.

When people look at you when speaking to you, and when you take the time to look at people when speaking to them, it is a form of respect. Take the time; look 'em in the eye … that person will know you mean it and care enough to really listen.

Tip 42
Walk a Mile in Their Shoes

Something that's really helped me understand my kids better is stopping and really thinking about their situation, putting myself in their shoes and trying to imagine what life must be like for them as they go through different experiences. I try to imagine how I would feel if this or that happened to me, and think up possible solutions to their problems.

I ask myself how I would feel if my very best friend from kindergarten on, after all those years, didn't want to talk to me when we both started Grade 7. How would I feel if I were being rushed and told several things at a time that I should be doing or needed to do, or how would I feel if I were told to do my homework, and asked if I had packed my lunch yet? etc., etc. ...

When you put yourself in your children's shoes, it gives you a better understanding of what they are dealing with and how they might be feeling about things. This brings better understanding and a strengthened relationship between parent and child.

Conclusion

I know how challenging it is to be a parent in today's world: I live it every day! I sincerely hope you find a few tips in this book helpful as you meet the challenges of parenting your own children. Use these tips consistently, have fun with them, and with your children!

If I can be of any service or support to you, please contact me at: sue@stuff4families.com and let me know.

Check out my website for more information on parenting and support: www.stuff4families.com

Be blessed.

Warmly,
Sue

Here are a couple of perspectives on parenting that I really like and that I thought you might also enjoy ...

Cost of Parenthood

The government recently calculated the cost of raising a child from birth to 18, and came up with $160,140 for a middle-income family. Talk about sticker shock. That doesn't even touch college tuition.

For those with kids, that figure leads to wild fantasies about all the things we could have bought, all the places we could have travelled, all the money we could have banked.

For others, that number might confirm the decision to remain childless. But $160,140 isn't so bad, if you break it down. It translates into $8,896.66 a year, $741.38 a month or $171.08 a week. That's a mere $24.44 a day.

Just over a dollar an hour.

Still, you might think the best financial advice would be not to have children if you want to be rich. It's just the opposite.

What do you get for your $160,140?

- Naming rights. First, middle and last.
- Glimpses of God every day.
- Giggles under the covers every night.
- More love than your heart can hold.

- Butterfly kisses and Velcro hugs.
- Endless wonder over rocks, ants, clouds and warm cookies.
- A hand to hold, usually covered with jam.
- A partner for blowing bubbles, flying kites, building sand castles and skipping down the sidewalk in the pouring rain.
- Someone to laugh yourself silly with no matter what the boss said or how your stocks performed that day.
- For $160,140, you never have to grow up. You get to finger paint, carve pumpkins, play hide-and-seek, catch lightning bugs and never stop believing in the impossible.
- You have an excuse to keep reading the adventures of Piglet, Pooh, and Tigger too, watching Saturday morning cartoons, going to Disney movies and wishing on stars.
- You get to frame rainbows, hearts, and flowers under refrigerator magnets and collect spray-painted noodle wreaths for Christmas, handprints set in clay for Mother's Day and cards with backward letters for Father's Day.
- For $160,140, there's no greater bang for your buck. You get to be a hero just for retrieving a Frisbee off the garage roof, taking the training wheels off the bike, removing a sliver, filling the wading pool, coaxing a wad of gum out of bangs and coaching a baseball team that never wins but always gets treated to ice cream regardless.
- You get a front-row seat to history to witness the first step, first word, first bra, first date, first time behind the wheel.

- You get to be immortal.
- You get another branch added to your family tree, and if you're lucky, a long list of limbs in your obituary called grandchildren.
- You get an education in psychology, nursing, criminal justice, communications and human sexuality no college can match.
- In the eyes of a child, you rank right up there with God. You have the power to heal a booboo, scare away monsters under the bed, patch a broken heart, police a slumber party, ground them forever and love them without limits, so one day they will, like you, love without counting the cost.

writer unknown

And another perspective ...

Mean Moms

Someday when my children are old enough to understand the logic that motivates a parent, I will tell them:

- I loved you enough ... to ask where you were going, with whom, and what time you would be home.

- I loved you enough ... to insist that you save your money and buy a bike for yourself even though we could afford to buy one for you.

- I loved you enough ... to be silent and let you discover that your new best friend was a creep.

- I loved you enough ... to make you go pay for the bubble gum you had taken and tell the clerk, "I stole this yesterday and want to pay for it."

- I loved you enough ... to stand over you for two hours while you cleaned your room, a job that should have taken 15 minutes.

- I loved you enough ... to let you see anger, disappointment and tears in my eyes. Children must learn that their parents aren't perfect.

- I loved you enough ... to let you assume the responsibility for your actions even when the penalties were so harsh they almost broke my heart.

- But most of all, I loved you enough ... to say NO when I knew you would hate me for it.

Those were the most difficult battles of all. I'm glad I won them, because in the end you won, too.

And someday when your children are old enough to understand the logic that motivates parents, you will tell them ...

Was your Mom mean?

- I know mine was. We had the meanest mother in the whole world! While other kids ate candy for breakfast, we had to have cereal, eggs, and toast.

- When others had a Pepsi and a Twinkie for lunch, we had to eat sandwiches.

- And you can guess our mother fixed us a dinner that was different from what other kids had, too.

- Mother insisted on knowing where we were at all times. You'd think we were convicts in a prison.

- She had to know who our friends were, and what we were doing with them.

- She insisted that if we said we would be gone for an hour, we would be gone for an hour or less.

- We were ashamed to admit it, but she had the nerve to break the Child Labor Laws by making us work.

- We had to wash the dishes, make the beds, learn to cook, vacuum the floor, do laundry, empty the trash and all sorts of cruel jobs. I think she would lie awake at night thinking of more things for us to do.

- She always insisted on us telling the truth the whole truth, and nothing but the truth. By the time we were teenagers, she could read our minds. Then, life was really tough!

- Mother wouldn't let our friends just honk the horn when they drove up. They had to come up to the door so she could meet them.

- While everyone else could date when they were 12 or 13, we had to wait until we were 16.

- Because of our mother we missed out on lots of things other kids experienced.

- None of us have ever been caught shoplifting, vandalizing other's property or ever arrested for any crime.

It was all her fault. Now that we have left home, we are all educated, honest adults. We are doing our best to be mean parents just like Mom was.

I think that is what's wrong with the world today.

It just doesn't have enough mean moms.

writer unknown

Give the Gift of Extraordinary Books

ORDER HERE using this form.

YES, I want to order the book *Raising Well-Behaved Kids*.

_____ Copies   @ $20.00   CDN/US = _____

Shipping and Handling:

$3.50 for the first item and $3.00 for each additional item. Shipping & handling amounts are the same whether paying in Canadian or US Dollars.

1st Item	=	$3.50
_____ Additional Items @ $3.00	=_____	
Order Sub-Total		_____
Canadian Orders add 6% GST		_____
Total Order	========	

My cheque or money order payable to Sue Kruszewski for
$_____ CDN or US (circle one) is enclosed.

Please ship book(s) to the following:

Name: _____

Street: _____

City_____ Prov/State:_____

Postal/Zip Code: _____

Additional contact information (optional)

Phone: (_____)_____

Fax: (_____)_____

E-mail Address: _____

Mail this form with cheque or money order to:

My5 Publishing
4703 15A Avenue
Edmonton, Alberta
T6L 6J1

For further information
E-mail: sue@stuff4families.com